It's all about Jesus

Fr Pat

I *live now,*

not I

Life as it is now

becomes the mystery of Love in Christ

Father Pat McNulty

MADONNA HOUSE PUBLICATIONS
Combermere, Ontario, Canada

Madonna House Publications®
2888 Dafoe Rd, RR 2
Combermere ON K0J 1L0

www.madonnahouse.org/publications

I _live now_, not I

by Father Patrick McNulty

First Edition

First printing, January 1st—Feast of the Mother of God

Design by Rosalie McPhee Douthwright

Library and Archives Canada Cataloguing in Publication Data

McNulty, Patrick, 1931-

I live now, not I : Life as it is now becomes the mystery of Love in Christ / Pat McNulty.

ISBN 978-1-897145-52-4

1. Spiritual Life—Catholic Church. I. Title.

BX2350.3.M36 2008   248.4'82   C2007-907444-8

Dedicated to a very special Woman who loves to dress up in the sun, stand on the moon, wear stars around Her head, (Rv 12:1) and then, at random, appears to people all over the world.

Contents

Foreword

Whether we think of ourselves as saints or sinners it is ultimately our personal human condition with all its warts and wonders which shapes the radical union we have with Christ as a result of Baptism—in the flesh!   And, it is at the heart of the Christian adventure for us to discover all the personal connections we have through this union with Christ, moment by moment, day by day, past, present or future—in the flesh!

How is that possible if I am such a sinner, such a spiritual coward, so burdened by the guilt or shame of my own failures, so confined by the depression and despair of the world where I have to live, or so tired of the struggle, of the constant falling-down and getting up?   How? Through our everyday life!   It is through our everyday life, now a baptismal mystery, that " ... *slowly, God takes you by the hand, deeper, deeper, deeper, until you reach the bottom. And then you can see ... from the other side ... "*[1]

See what?   See that Christ desires, with the passion of a Heart that is "sacred," to bring us into the fullness of this "priesthood of the baptized," where we will finally understand that nothing in

---

1   Catherine Doherty. Local Directors' Meetings, 1963-80, Excerpt 21, September, 1976, pg. 348. (Unpublished.)

our life is wasted, not our past sins or our present woundedness.   Because through Baptism "I live, no longer I, but Christ lives in me"! (Gal 2:20)

Is that possible for the likes of me?

Come!   Let us ask the Lord and see where the Spirit takes us!

Prologue

Once Upon A Time ...

an old man died and went to "Hell"—or *Thereabouts*. He was deeply grieved and sorry though it seemed a just desert for he had never really loved God as fully as he was able or his neighbour as he ought. Now Death had "thieved" him too and he had come to naught.

As soon as he arrived *There* the howling creatures who inhabited *That Place* set about to mock and scorn him with loathing and disgust: "Your religious mumbo-jumbo will cease soon enough when it becomes as useless in Eternity as it was in Time."

Eternity did indeed wear on but so too the old man's endless cry. It so upset everyone *There* that they pushed him down, ever deeper down, until he reached a depth where few had ever been—so deep it seemed outside *That Place*. And then one night—there are no days *There*—his cry ceased and he was never seen or heard from again. They say that the same Angel Who accompanied Christ from *That Place* still waits *There* for those simple souls who pass by with His Name ever on their lips and carries them away.

Or so they say ...

Introduction

When you are as old as I am (pushing 80) and you are trying to chronicle your journey of Faith, those major spiritual moments of your "piece of history," it's no surprise to discover that someone else has already done it and has perhaps done it better than you can. But it is stimulating to discover that those who have done it have had insights and experiences so similar to yours that it would almost seem they had secretly broken into your room, tore the pages out of your journal, and plagiarized them as their own. Such was the case when I recently re-read a lovely little book by Fr. Gerald Vann, O.P., titled *The Pain of Christ and the Sorrow of God*. (Fr. Vann was a popular Dominican priest who wrote extensively between 1930 and 1963.) I wouldn't have had a clue what he was talking about if I had read it when he wrote it in 1947, but 50 years later I had more than just a "clue" for I discovered, in a few short paragraphs, the outline of my whole journey, in words better than any I could have penned myself.

In 1947, two years after the end of WW II, when Fr. Vann wrote that book, I was 16 years old. I thought the world was mine for the taking, "my oyster" as we would say. Life in North America was upward, outward, and filled with endless possibility. But by the time I was 40, things had changed drastically—at least for me. What I had imagined in the 60's to be a new and hope-filled vision of faith and life slipped away like "a dream dies at the break of day."

In the 60's people were calling any degree of spiritual/emotional darkness, dryness or aridity "the dark night of the soul" *à la* St. John of the Cross as if it were a temporary power outage in the left or right brain. Well, mine was not the classic "dark night" of John of the Cross—or at least I don't think so, primarily because it seemed so self-inflicted. But from that tradition I knew that what was happening to me was intimately yoked to the journey of Faith regardless of the psychological or historical causes. I knew that on this journey one could lose his immortal soul, but I felt that if I was not to lose my mind I needed a sign and no sign seemed forthcoming.

> *"They once asked the Lord for a sign, and he told them that a sign should not be given them except the sign of Jonas the prophet. For pride, for self-sufficiency, for the righteousness of conventionalized piety, there can be no other sign than that ... pride will never learn what Christianity means until it has gone down into the darkness, until it is left naked and helpless and without resources and so is thrown back into the arms of*

God ... If we were wise we could learn this for ourselves. But we are stupid; and sometimes God has to force it on our attention ..."[2]

I had been one of those Christians who believed that Faith was always upward movement, a forward call in the world to better and more productive things with art, music, and literature to guide and delight us along the way out of our own personal human circumstances. Consequently I did not pay that much attention to the heritage of my Catholic spirituality which proclaimed that we must also eventually face the burdens and pains of our own personal human condition, often left "unhealed by God," and in that darkness was a key to Joy. I had forgotten that the central focus of the whole Christian mystery is the Incarnation—God "in the human condition"—and because I had forgotten that, the other Faith-things of mind and heart gradually became opaque and obscure. In the theological twilight that remained, faith was more and more uncertain for me, and my beloved Church, with its seeming lack of response to the real issues of the day, was now a scandal to me, as very soon I became a scandal to myself. In that psychologically charged atmosphere, unex-

2   Gerald Vann, O.P., *The Pain of Christ and the Sorrow of God.* Blackfriars Publication, Oxford, 1947, pgs. 44-47.

plained memories began to loom up in my psyche and suddenly my early childhood became fearsome and bewildering. And then one day I woke up and I could see nothing at all—I was in total spiritual darkness, and my life was a disaster.

> "*Sometimes God in his pity uses a disaster of one sort or another precisely to sweep away all our illusions and bring us back to reality. It may be a terrible moral collapse that shakes us to our roots; it may be a loss of faith, of faith in God, of faith in ourselves, of faith in everything; it may be the pressure of external events, the collapse of a world about our ears: in one way or another we can be left naked, we begin to see ourselves as we really are in our nothingness; we go down into the darkness; and there in that darkness we begin to cry, 'Out of the depths;' (Ps. 130) and then at last there is hope for us ... "[3]*

This journey "*out of the depths*" of our own human condition is not singular to Christianity, but there is a very particular incline on the road as a Christian travels, a very special pattern to what happens to them along the way, and a very exacting focus if they want to "see" and know

---

3   Vann, Ibid.

God as they travel.   The personal events of the life of a Christian are not what define the journey, nor are the social and political issues which are often highlighted for them along the way. The focus is that which has been happening personally between them and God from the moment of their conception, but especially the moment of their baptism into the life of the incarnate Son of God—in the flesh!   And however their own life is put together, by whatever faithful or fateful means it unfolds, if they are not clear about this unique and ofttimes unfamiliar union with Christ, then they travel without joy and live without hope. And there is nothing more frightful than a Christian without joy or hope. Just ask me!

We must all come to a moment, even if only in death, when we are swallowed up by the mystery of Life, of the human condition, of our own personal circumstance, caught perhaps by some foolish or unfortunate choice, or some nasty, odious accident. With our earthly eyes we can no longer see, and with our mortal minds we can no longer comprehend because there is nothing left to see or comprehend: there is only God and me. And one day, only God! But it is then that the Spirit can make us privy to the secret of the whole Christian life—to each of us with our own warts and wonders.   That secret is our union with the Son of God, in the flesh, *as we are now*!

Not how we could be or should be—that comes later—but how we are now! Saints or sinners. We each have our own "threads" with which we weave together our everyday life of Faith, but the needle which draws them into a pattern is that simple affair of life by which we are finally pierced by the inevitable weakness of our own human condition and discover within it the mysterious design and joyful presence of God in the flesh, in my flesh, from the very beginning but especially since Baptism.

> *"There is no way to life except through death and re-birth ... [and] the death that leads to resurrection is not just a death, but a sacrificial death, a death turned into an act of love and self-giving. You have your pain and your sorrow, your anxieties, your personal problems, your moral lapses, perhaps your loss of faith ... It may be a moral abyss from which you feel yourself wholly impotent to escape; it may be a sense of utter blankness: a loss of the faith that once explained life and made it happy, so that now everything seems meaningless. These states can sometimes be due to physical or mental exhaustion, essentially transitory: that does not mean that while they exist they are any the less real. But if they come to you, refuse to despair: it may well be that*

this death is your way of life. Refuse to despair, and be comforted: it may well be that this death is the way which God's love has discovered for you of finding, not the unreal conventionalized Christ who leaves your egoism intact, but the real Christ, the Christ on the Cross, the Christ who is Love. Refuse to despair, and on the contrary ... put your very dereliction itself into his hands ... turn these into the sign of Jonas the prophet, use these to lead you down into the darkness, take these to the altar of love and tumble them into his hands and ask him to deal with them, like a little child taking a worthless piece of treasure trove as a gift to its mother. And not your own sorrows and your own sins merely, but the sorrows and sins of the world: you who should be so powerful to heal then in the might of Love and who in fact are so powerless to do anything, take these too and give them to him, make these too an act of sacrificial love, suffering for them yourself in union with his sorrow ; and so, having seen to the very depths of your own ineffectiveness, you will cease to be ineffective. You will begin to live, now not you, but Christ living in you...and sooner perhaps than you could hope, more richly certainly than you could dream, he will turn those waters of sorrow into the rich red wine of life."[4]

My own journey into the *"waters of sorrow"* is perhaps a bit severe, sometimes even a mite depressing, but *"sooner perhaps than you could hope, more richly certainly than you could dream, He will turn those waters of sorrow into the rich red wine of life."* And even if it does take a lifetime to get there, it's a journey worth spending a lifetime on.

---

4   Vann, Ibid.

1   Born Again

"What precisely is this chain of acts and events that runs from our first hour through our last? ... The God who made you, saved you , and will one day place you in his light, also directs your life. What happens between birth and death is message, challenge, test, succor—all from his hands. It is not meant to be learned theoretically, but personally experienced and assimilated ... Until a man makes this transposition he will have no peace ... " [5]

I have had a very fruitful though often fitfully difficult 76 years shaped by an Irish-European ancestry, lived out in North America, and set in that more ancient Judaeo-Christian history. Yet, it was only in the last twenty-five years, in the midst of many a dreadful bout of doubts and fears and life-long depression, in that land "between sin and sanctity," that I suddenly saw clearly the powerful mystery and hidden joy of my own human condition and how it is the very source of union with Christ and not some neurotic state to be rid of.

---

5   Romano Guardini, *The Lord.*   Gateway Editions, Ltd., South Bend, Indiana, 1954, Chapter 12, Part Four, pgs. 295, 297.

This new vista of hope did not open up all at once; it was well-rooted in decades of my beloved Catholic tradition and many happy years as priest. But when it happened it was clear all at once! There were no grace-games— "I'll do this if you do that, God." Nor was there any high-powered healing, miracles, conversion experiences, altar-calls, et al. There were no heroic fasts and foodless days and nights. There was only the burdensome journey through life day by day by day by day. And for years the pain was so intense I could not let it out and even if I had I wouldn't have known what to do with it: Faith had become the problem and not the answer. My only option was silence.

In the beginning it was not the silence of going away from all the external noise and confusion, a man-made solitude, but rather that normal silence which is created when we are finally face-to-face with all the unanswered questions. I think that silence began for me in earnest when I found the need for professional therapy back in 1967, and this eventually led me into actual solitude, a cabin in the woods—but more of that later. The questions I had early on were all about the common struggle with the issues of the day often made more intense by one's own height-ened social and emotional involvement. Out of that awareness we are led to ponder such things as: "Does my life really make any difference?" or

"Can we really change anything?" Then when the door to the Psyche begins to open a crack the bigger questions loom, "What is the purpose of Life?" "Who am I?" Questions. Questions. Questions. But the very *unanswered-ness* of the questions eventually wears us down and points us to solitude, to a solitude that is a going away from all the external noise and confusion in us and around us—whether we go away regularly for short periods of time, or finally for a long period of time.

If we stay in that solitude long enough we will learn why silence wrapped itself around us in the first place. For it is in silence that we discover the journey is not a cerebral or psychological one in which all the questions are asked and finally answered. Nor is it a mantra mode by which the painful matters of life are hummed away by sheer spiritual discipline. Rather, silence is a strange, wordless soul-place where there are no more answers because there are no more questions! And that is the beginning of solitude!

Silence is about us. Solitude is about God. But if we let silence do its job it will lead us into solitude. And in that solitude we enter the heart of our own personal history, our own human situation, and face the sometimes-appalling mystery that everything in our life is either about a personal relationship with a personal God or, everything in our life is about nothing at all and so are we!   It is in solitude, of whatever form, that we come head-on to the inherent paradox of our own personal faith-life: Does Christ bring me any real hope and joy in the midst of my pain, my situation, my fears, my sins, my mistakes, my illness, my broken heart as I am now—perhaps sad not happy, depressed not delighted, in sin not sanctity? Does He?

In solitude God "speaks" in different ways to each person because each one's path is different and each life-experience is unique. But what God "says" is meant to take each one of us into the very heart of our own humanity and thus into the humanity of Christ. This is universal for the Christian! This *is* the journey! And on that journey everything familiar must succumb to the darkness of faith until there is only Him and me left. And finally, only Him! That is solitude!

To those depths few of us go until some unusual circumstances of life force us. *"If we were wise we could learn this for ourselves. But we are stupid; and sometimes God has to force it on our attention ... "*[6] Indeed, most of the time we imagine that our own Christian fidelity empowers us to re-write the script of the human condition on our own terms with our own vision of Life. We have forgotten that the primary journey of the faith-full

---

6 Vann, op.cit.

Christian is to finally meet the God Who **is** vs. the lesser god we often create for ourselves, to finally see our life as it really is vs. the fantasy we have often created in the name of faith or religion. As God dismantles that fantasy, our own personal human circumstance seems like a huge stone that rolls across the doorway of our faith and locks us in some new tomb. And yet, with the fantasy broken, we meet Christ there in His human circumstance. He rolls away the stone and carries us away!

So it was that the familiar Church and State for which I had poured out my life for over forty years died in the early 70's as far as I was concerned—a very painful death leaving me in a frightening tomb. The theology and politics which formed my life had fallen away and I felt betrayed by the very ones who had taught it to me so well. The religious and political sins of the past, mine and history's, began to catch up with me and hounded me to the edge of some darkness I did not understand; and yet so many seemed to have had some other faith-persuasion by which they could explain it all away and get on with their lives, whereas I had nothing. Finally I could find no peace unless I entered a place of physical solitude for longer periods of time to face all these pressing unanswered questions about my country, my church, morality, freedom, God, healing—oh yes, especially the questions about healing!

I began to spend extended periods of time alone in a cabin in the wilds at Madonna House in Combermere, Ontario, Canada. It was just a simple place—they called it *poustinia*, a Russian word for "desert." There was no electricity or plumbing; there was a make-shift bed, a wood stove, a chair and table, a large wooden cross on the wall and a bible. The rest was between you and God! And the first day I ever went there I started right out on God!

> "*Everyone and their dog claims healing from You Lord, but you never heal me. I just go on and on and on in this darkness with little hope or joy—just raw faith. I believe in You—Yes, you are 'my personal saviour'—and when I fail I repent and move on in hope. I am constantly nourished on Your Word and Your Body and Blood. But, where are you? In my life? Now? Really?*"

Silence!

> "*Lord, You were born into the human condition, took on my life in the flesh, but what difference does that make to my personal human condition, here, now, in my everyday life on this earth? The Incarnation changed everything but it hasn't changed*

my human condition. The pain grows, the darkness is darker, and I am closer to my grave. Where does that leave me? What is my life all about, Lord?"

Silence!

I wasn't surprised that I did not "hear" any answers so early on, because I already knew that solitude is meant to cut between the marrow and the bone of mere questions and answers. But we are meant to "hear" something in the solitude —and this is what I heard?

"It is only in the solitude that I can gain your attention and capture your heart, Patrick. And I so need you right now!"

*"What the hell kind of an answer is that, Lord? Number one: I am your creature, You are my God, so You have my attention all the time. And, number two: what do you mean, You need me? What about **me**?"*

Silence. More and more silence.

And then one night when I lit my candle before the image of His face, as I was often wont to do there, and sat down in the shadows and the pain, the solitude took me into some place deep in me where I had never allowed myself to go before:

"You tell me, Lord, that You love me. You tell me to trust You. So then, answer me this:

where were You when I was being so abused
as a young lad? Where were You when I
cried out as I have so often since? You had
my full attention. And I surely needed You!
Now You come to me telling me that you
want my attention and that You need me! I
beg Your pardon! You wonna run that one
by me again?"

There is a fine line between truth and blasphemy and I was getting closer to blasphemy all the time. And then it seemed to me that He spoke again.

"It was not you who was being abused,
Patrick. It was Me. I am the One who
bears the pain of the whole world, of
everyone, saint and sinner, until the end
of time. That's the mystery of the
Incarnation. That's the meaning of
Love! I am one with the abused and the
abuser!"

Solitude had done its job well: if I had "heard" these words in my heart only a few years earlier I probably would have chalked them up to some psychotic episode, or useless mumbo-jumbo; I would have completed the blasphemy and been finished with religion altogether. But now I was utterly dumb-struck. I could not put two words together in response. I sat there looking at the picture of His face and began to weep. (Did He weep too?)

> *"I look for every possible way to show each one the depth of this union which begins at the moment of conception, and is made final in baptism. It is a union meant for all the Baptized, saints and sinners. It is my personal mercy to each and everyone, my personal love. And I thirst for those who believe it and come to me through it. Come and be with me. I need you as you are. I need you! I love you!"*

That night I sat before His Face for hours just repeating His Name over and over and over. I could not fathom what He had "said." All I could do was indulge in the new passion and soak up the joy—it had been a long long time since I had known joy with any passion! The only sound that broke the silence was the sound of His Name being repeated over and over, a habit which I had embraced through the Jesus Prayer many years before and had never ceased saying it since.

Incidently, this is not a chronicle about sexual abuse. We each have our individual, personal circumstances which point us to Christ and it is our task to let them lead us there regardless! The causes and effects of all the sins from our earliest years, everything from family wounding, ecclesiastical wantonness, or neuroses of all kinds must indeed be taken very seriously but they are not ultimately determinative. They do affect us and perhaps even leave us broken or wounded all of our lives—be we victims or predators. But as Christians we cannot understand or explain our life in the contemporary terminology of that human condition.

The ultimate purpose of the human condition, our own situation, the reason why we are left wounded or unhealed, is to take us into the mystery of that union in Christ which is common to all the baptized, and to somehow see that with the eyes of Christ. After we go there and live there for a long time, even if in our own sinfulness and great shame, *then* we can get the connection between us and Him, and *then* we can talk about justice and responsibility. Until then most of us are in denial and pointing fingers at everybody else. I certainly was.

But, is it possible that everything which happens to us is the instrument by which He Himself draws us into His wounded heart through our own human condition—whatever it is or however we got there? Is it He who first suffers the pain we suffer, He who makes Himself one with us in our pain so we will not die from the pain or in the darkness? Is He one with me as I am right now? Is that what love is—His for me and mine for Him? Is it possible that, *"what happens between birth and death is—all from his hands?"*[7]

If so, then why do all the wounds and weaknesses seem to remain at least in some shadow form? Why have we not found some holy herb with which to heal the memory of all our personal sins and those historical wounds, those terrible things we never dreamed we Christians were capable of? I don't know. All I know is that something simple and wonderful happened to my heart after so many years of solitude, and I didn't have to do anything but humbly stand in the blinding light of the mystery of my own darkness, my own human condition as it is right now, with Him in it right now.

It makes no difference how we come to these holy moments on the journey, even if by our own foolish choices or dreadful sins. All that matters is that we are here, helpless, perhaps even hopeless and totally vulnerable. And because, in our best biblical spirituality, we believe that whatever we do to anyone else, including myself, we also do to Christ, and thus somehow to all human beings, then have we not all been abusers too—abusers of others and of Christ? Yes, we must plummet those depths, down, down, ever deeper down until we realize that we are all abused and we are all abusers if

---

7   Guardini, op.cit.

the Gospel is our measure!   And only in the awesome environment of such Truth can we hear Christ speak to us heart-to-heart and finally convince us, saint or sinner:

> *"You and I are one. You must not look anywhere else for the meaning to your pain or darkness, no matter what the sin or the consequence of it. Come into my Heart through yours and I will show you everything. All I need is a heart pierced by its own human condition just like Mine has been pierced, a heart that has no place else to go but to My heart. I will do the rest."*

Only God can say and do things like that: this is not psychology, or even mere spirituality, but Grace formed by Revelation. This is the blessed shock of experiencing a oneness with Christ which begins the healing and brings the joy and hope we have always sought but thought we were too much of a failure or too great a sinner to have. This then the *"chain of acts and events that runs from our first hour through our last: this the message, challenge, test, succor—all from his hands ... not meant to be learned theoretically, but personally experienced and assimilated ...* [for until we] *make this transposition he will have no peace."*[8]

---

8   Guardini, ob cit.

2   Back to Eden

"But the serpent said to the woman: "You certainly will not die! No, God knows well that the moment you eat of it your eyes will be opened and you will be like gods, who know what is good and what is bad." (Gn 3: 4-5)

Imagine that your deepest pain and fear, your deepest anger, your shattered dreams and hidden terrors, all your disappointment, your greatest sadness in life, especially as little children, imagine that it all points to God, personally, and that it is somehow all from God's hands.   And then consider that the consequent behaviour which flows from all those events and wounds in your life from the very beginning   also falls within God's providence, and is also somehow from God's hands. Would not many be tempted to ask, "What kind of God are you?" I did.

We Christians are told, of course, that the essential resolution to these pressing questions about our personal lives is to be found in the mystery of Original Sin. Truth be told, I was never quite satisfied with the Original Sin "thing" myself.   I don't mean theologically or biblically but emotionally. I always felt like "damaged goods," that I was missing something essential to life itself from the moment of my conception.   I felt victimized because I had to bear in my soul and psyche all the deadly effects of the actions of two folk in a Garden whom I never knew or met. And, as if that were not enough, after you're baptized the responsibility is exponential. Not only do I have to deal with a womb-disadvantage during my whole lifetime on earth because of this Original Sin, but if I ain't careful I could end up in a tomb-disadvantage forever! "Original Sin? I didn't do anything. Why should I have to answer for somebody else's sin? What kind of a God are you!?"

Blasphemy? Not quite. Because here we find ourselves at the entrance of one of those essential theological impasses which we must break through, an emotional wasteland that is so deep in our soul, our psyche, it often feels as if we have suddenly wandered out into the desert and will die there. Yet it is here, in this desert of Faith, this garden-wasteland where we finally understand the satanic hiss which has been robbing us of our rightful inheritance from the moment of our Baptism. And even though our best tradition is there to guide us through this desert most of us feel like we have to figure it all out on our own. Why?

> *"Pride will never learn what Christianity means until it has gone down into the darkness, until it is left naked and helpless and*

*without resources and so is thrown back into
the arms of God ... If we were wise we could
learn this for ourselves. But we are stupid;
and sometimes God has to force it on our
attention ... "9*

I didn't figure that out until the silence drove me
all the way into a cave in the Sinai desert. Of
course, it was not necessary to trek into the Sinai
to find an answer because the desert is actually
a place in every human heart where we are
exposed to all the deadly elements of soul and
psyche with the minimum of life-essentials with
which to protect our Self, where emotional and
theological mirages flourish and delude us,
tempt us to wander every-which-way in the heat
of the struggle. But there is new life in That
Place. We must go There and walk in the heat of
the day with the God Who Is vs. the god we have
fashioned, if we are to find that new life, knowing full-well that if needlessly exposed There for
too long, Faith can die and with it Hope and
Love.

I don't know what I expected to find out there in
the Sinai desert in a mountain-cave miles from
any other human being, and if at first I was
deluded into thinking "the Lord called me" for
great and holy things, that delusion was defunct
in less than a 48 hours. By then the first wave of

---

9 Vann, ob cit.

terror had swept over me to remind me that here I was in a place where I had no defences at all. I suddenly realized that it was not only my soul I could lose out here but I could also lose my mind as well. Then what?

Well, eventually we realize that we do not go out into any desert on our own but it is the Lord who lures us into the wilderness to speak to our hearts. (Hos 2:14) And what did He speak?

> "**It is time for you to face your own part in original sin and stop playing hide-and-seek with Me in the Garden of your heart!**"

> "*I didn't commit any original sin—at least nothing so original that it affects my whole life like The Original Sin.*"

> "**Yes you did. And you do it over and over everyday.**"

> "*What?*"

> "**You do not believe that my hand is in every incident of your personal life, even the unhealed effects of your sins? Why are you so sad that your life does not proceed as you think it should? And why are you so hopeless at how your life has turned out? You are angry. And your anger is directed at Me because I am God and you are not!**"

"I've never wanted to be God!   I may have some problems with what kind of God you are at times but I certainly don't want to be You!"

"But you do not believe me.   You refuse to believe that the chain of acts and events that runs from your first hour through your last is all from My hands. You keep eating from the tree in the Garden so that YOU can go on deciding what YOU think is best and what is not best for you in your life!   You still want to be God.   That's the original sin!   And that is my grief: it deprives you of the knowledge of the union we already have together, the one you are still looking for!"

Obviously that sin is not as exceptional as the Original one in the Garden but it is a mutual one and one that seldom figures in our neat moral categories. And yet, is it not at the foundation of all our other sins, this lack of trust in God's personal presence in our lives now? It is for me. And I knew I was getting close to the "original" when I heard myself cry out, *"What kind of God are you?"* That question has different patterns in each of our lives but in the end it is all there in our personal history.

Our everyday life will eventually bring it out:

"What kind of God are you?"

"Why did my life turn out this way?

"Where were you when my babies all died of starvation?

"Where were you when I was conceived with AIDS?

"Why did you weave this particular psyche and soul together without my own free choice with all these ancestral wounds and weakness stamped in my DNA leading to such a burdensome life?

"Where were you when the tsunami wiped out every living relative of mine?

"Where were you when childhood abuse drowned me in fear and despair?

"Where were you when I went blind at 10 because we couldn't afford simple medication— a dollar a week—and your Christian minions had millions to spend on junk.

"Where were you when I couldn't find a job to even support my family and ended up on the street?

"Where were you when I was ready to have a family and then had to go off to War and die?"

"What kind of God are you?"

Whether we use those words or not there is some disturbingly "unfinished business" between us and our God—not between God and us, that's why it is called "sin." It is unfinished because, whether we know it or accept it, our deepest pain and fear, our deepest anger and disappointment is ultimately directed at God, personally. We may live it out on other people or ourselves but the primary target is God! We have to recognize that and deal with it or we cannot be healed of the effects of our own part in Original Sin.

We have to realize that our shattered dreams and hidden terrors, even as little children, are all about a disappointment between us and God, personally! Our own malicious behaviour, rabid or moderate, personal or historical, is ultimately "payback" directed at God personally for what we deem to have been God's absence in our lives when God should have been present. But, if God is God, and I am not, then all these things have their ultimate meaning and purpose in God and not in me, not in my personal life, not even in the history of the human condition. If God is God and I am not then *"the chain of acts and events that runs from* (my) *first hour through* (my) *last* (is) *all from his hands ... "*[10]

***

10   Guardini, ob cit.

God is God! I am not! In our blessed Christian tradition when we say that it is not demeaning, self-condemning or a harbinger of shame and guilt; rather does it make way for the fruitfulness of the Joy that sets us free!   For in the awe-full desert silence and solitude of every human heart we are meant to discover that original answer to our own "original" sin. And when it becomes the life-giving answer to all our questions, whether historical or personal, then we can return to the Garden and once again walk with God to the tree of Life because, once again in my life, "God is God and I am not!" Then we can enter into the presence of God as Father, Son and Holy Spirit, who are persons and not dispassionate anthropological myths or tacky scientific bangs.

Our tradition reveals God as person, and now in Christ, One who knows our own human condition, in the flesh, unlike any other god.   Now we can know in the depths of our soul and body what the human condition really is all about, what it really means, and the joy each of us is meant to have, whether we are still sequestered and struggling in our own desert cave, or dancing out the mysterious possibilities of a theophany on the top of the mountain.

In the desert this whole mystery of Original Sin falls into place and the last figment of false freedom that leads to death is peeled away. We begin to realize that we have already joined Adam and Eve in that Original Sin for in whatever way we do not envision God intertwined and involved in every moment of our lives, good, bad or indifferent, we are listening to the same satanic hiss. In whatever way we do not sit quietly in the solitude of our own mysterious human situation as it is now, and let Christ reveal to us the meaning of our lives in Him, now, we are being "original" again in our own sin. And as long as we have to be so damn original He cannot take us to the tree of life in the interior of our own baptized heart and soul.

These are strange times in which we live. Two thirds of the world are trapped in human conditions beyond our imagination. And little by little the ranks of those not abused, addicted, unwanted, abandoned or imprisoned grows smaller and smaller. As we move through our own short moment in contemporary history we too must learn how to embrace a whole new image of life and faith and all the questions that come with it. The human circumstances leading up to these questions are different for each but they all point in the same direction. And for most of us, our experience, our image of God is dreadfully terrestrial and materialistic, some socio-political investment as if now there is nothing we cannot do or become as a Christian! But as this fable unravels in our everyday life, we will become more and more aware of God's socio-political "absence." And eventually the day will come when, as an individual or a nation, we too will cry out once again, "Where were You when I needed You?" "Why did my life turn out this way?" "What kind of God are you?" Then the Spirit can lure us out into the desert where we can either rediscover the life-giving and essential truth about our Christian Faith, namely, that we and Christ are one in the flesh now, or else we can fashion for ourselves something more "original" and end up with nothing at all.

The Original Sin is indeed the deepest wound in our hearts but there is another similar to it that keeps us from the light of the Gospel. Christ Himself warns us that the most deadly personal wound of Original Sin is the sin against the Holy Spirit, that personal, culpable sin against a personal God. Not a behavioural sin—something I do—but a deadly attitude about a personal God Who loves and cares for me personally: "You were not there when I needed You." "I have been faithful to You all of my life and it didn't change anything." "I didn't do anything. Why should I have to answer for somebody else's sin?" "What kind of a God are you!?" These are the kinds of questions which betray our part in Original Sin! And it must be healed or we will die in the desert, and with that death goes Faith, Hope and Love.

I didn't have an Elijah experience (1 Kgs 19) in my desert even though I was in the same general vicinity where he had once been. And I don't know what Elijah really discovered in the gentle breeze that followed the wind, earthquake and fire, but I know what *I* discovered. I believe it was in the desert, in that seemingly desolate place in my own heart, where I finally discovered that Jesus delights to live there because it bespeaks the depths of His Own embrace of the human condition when He too took flesh. It is there, in our own flesh, that we are most like Him because it is there that He proves His most profound love of us in our own human condition and thus the love of His Father for each of us, in the flesh. Incredible.

What that eventually translates into in our everyday life is that Faith is not some kind of spirituality with which we pray or "ohm" ourselves out of the human condition, but it is the gradual unfolding of our own life after the fashion of the life, death and resurrection of the Son of God through our human condition, as it is now together with Him!

If we humbly and prayerfully go "into the desert," go into that mysterious silence of our own life, our own hearts, instead of into all the reasons why our life is such a mess and should have been different, we discover that it is God who has mercifully blocked our way with thorns, and walls us in and lures us out into the wilderness so He can speak to our hearts, as the Prophet says. And what does God speak there?

The prophet Hosea tells us that from the time we were a child, God loved us; it was God who taught us how to walk, took us in his arms, and like an infant close to the cheek, stooped down and gave us our food. *"How could I give you up? … my heart is overwhelmed, [and] my pity is stirred … for I am God and not man, the Holy One present among you …"* (Hos 11: 1, 3, 4, 8, 9)

We learn from this great Christian desert tradition that we can only look to Christ and Him alone for the meaning of our entire life, from its very beginning to its very end and beyond. Only He is the revelation of who God **is** and thus who I am not. But, even more significantly, the revelation of who I really am—one with the Son of God in the flesh. Who would have thought such a thing was possible?

Indeed, thank God that God is God and I am not!

3   On the Far Side of Pain

" ... you are one with Jesus ... All that is his is yours ...his breath in your breath, his heart in your heart, all the faculties of his soul in the faculties of your soul ... you have one breath with him, one soul, one life, one will, one mind, one heart ... He desires that whatever is in him may live and rule in you ...."[11]

If you are at all like me I can imagine what might be going through your mind about now: "It was nice what you did for us Jesus, but You had a perfect home, there were no drugs in your family, no robbers or thieves in your neighbourhood. You never went to prison. You were never abused. Your parents loved each other. You never had sibling rivalry. You were never the child of an alcoholic. You were not conceived with AIDS. You were never determined by the kinds of sins we commit. Yes, it was nice what you did for us, but it's not how I have to live."

How far from the truth such thinking is! But it's OK because it brings us deeper into the heart of the matter because Faith often breaks down

---

11   St. John Eudes, *On the Admirable Heart of Jesus.* Lib 1, 5: Opera Omnia 6. 113-115. (Liturgy of the Hours, Office of Readings, August 17.)

when our life seems to have no practical, real connection with the life of Christ at all, those darkest moments in our own situation when we cannot find anything in our lives to compare with His. "It was nice what you did for us Jesus but ... " And so, for many many people any kind of real and effective union with Christ through their own circumstances, their life as it is right now, is not realistic, not even impossible. "You never ... " "You never ... " "You never ... "

A faith dilemma indeed! And yet, it is at this very juncture on the journey when we are meant to cross over into the most incredible experience of personal union with Christ we can imagine. And it is here that many of our great saints, shored up with the teaching of the Church, cry out with reckless abandon that our life and His life are one now! Blaise Pascal wrote: *"Christ is in agony until the end of the world."*[12] No, Christ does not come to it by the same means we do, but if it is there in me then He is there in it. My task, my privilege is to seek Him there and embrace Him there, in my own human condition now, even if all of Hell is mocking me!

Christ said that what we do to the least we do to Him because He is one with them. But we seldom take that revelation to its complement,

---

12   Blaise Pascal, *"Pensées,"* n. 553 Br.

namely, what is done to me is done to Him because He and I are one too. " ... *you are one with Jesus ... All that is his is yours ... his breath in your breath, his heart in your heart, all the faculties of his soul in the faculties of your soul ... you have one breath with him, one soul, one life, one will, one mind, one heart .... He desires that whatever is in him may live and rule in you ...* "[13] Yes, but ...

No! We have to stop looking at our life through the veil of our own sins, our own personal history, our own present state in life, what we could have done, should have done, what we must yet do. We must take the risk, we must find Christ in our poor hearts now, as we are right now, no matter what. For if we wait for everything to be clear, perfect, right or holy we will never "get the connection" between Him and us. That's the whole point: we won't see the connection until we have no other explanation but union in Christ! Because only when we are so bereft of any other explanation can He show Himself to us in the flesh, through our flesh, through our own human situation now.

Yes, we must keep in mind that what Jesus experienced in His human condition was in no way clouded by the effects of personal sin like ours is.

---

13   Eudes, Ibid.

Because of this He had a clarity and presence to His human situations that we do not have. But we wrongly assume that to mean He is somehow separate from our experiences, or that He cannot know our pain as it comes to us, that He only knows it as God, clean and sinless. We rationalize: "Since He did not actually experience murder, war, addiction, or so many other things we could think of, then He cannot really affect my pain: He can be with me as one who cares for me, but He is always standing outside the circle of my pain looking in. It is nice, this pain that He suffered for me, but it is not mine. His is over and mine will go on until I die."

It is often at this moment that we pull back from the reality of our own human situation too soon and even try to explain it away spiritually: "Don't forget how much Jesus suffered for you." "Your pain is nothing compared to His." "He was the sinless Son of God but you were conceived a sinner—you're getting what you deserve." This is not the time to explain the reality of our own suffering or situation by putting it on a biblical or theological "scales" where the measure is between us sinful mortals and the sinless Son of God. Such measure will make the notion of union with Christ impossible! We have to enter the emotional and intellectual darkness and not come out too soon, not embrace a lesser answer to our pain and suffering than God's own—His

Son in our flesh! We have to let the pain do its thing on our soul, our psyche, our heart and our mind until things begin to break open naturally. I am thinking now of a very simple breaking-open-moment when I saw the photo of a little girl in the back seat of a car with her terrorized face pushed up against the window. She was being physically removed from her adoptive parents of many years because of a legal battle with the blood parents whom she did not even know. I weep when I remember the look of utter terror and abandonment on that poor little girl's face as that car was pictured driving her away to "new parents," taking her deep into a new pain in her life from which she may never pull through on this earth. I had never had her particular experience so where did all that oneness with the little girl come from?

Well, we know there is a unity in pain that is beyond the circumstances which cause it, and out of that common unity we are teased out of ourselves by the pain of others and thus we learn how to embrace each other and minister to each other in our pain—in a word, to feel compassion which is the beginning of caring, even if from a distance. And this kind of *natural* compassion begins to create a purity of heart which takes on the image of love. And the more compassionate we are, the less we need to have had the same experience in order to be present to another person in pain. For having embraced our own pain we have allowed it to teach us what we cannot learn in any other way, and then we can know and reach out to others through a mutual experience of pain itself! When two people in mutual pain meet they don't have to ask if the other person really knows their pain in the same way they do: reaching out is proof enough.

As our hearts are purified by our own pain and the pain of others, one day we look at the pain of Christ with new eyes and now His pain can teach us something beyond compassion. At first this new awareness of the pain of Christ is ever-so -much like the simple compassion we have for each other in our mutual pain, like mine for the little girl. But, whether we know it or not, the Lord Himself has been busy revealing something new in our flesh, a very important dimension of pain which changes our human capacity to embrace the pain of others and gives us a healing power beyond mere compassion. For in compassion we have learned that even though we may not have come to our pain by the same human experiences or conditions as others to whom we reach out, in Christ it is suddenly mysteriously possible to *be* the pain of the other without having had their specific experiences which cause their pain. This new experience of pain is the beginning of union with the other, the beginning of Love beyond mere compassion.

This new gift of union, this "becoming the pain of the other" even though we have not come to it as they did, this is what we do not understand about Christ's revelation to us in the Gospels. He is telling us that there is a new, intimate, almost ontological unity between us and Him which is so real that what is done to us is done to Him and vice versa. Such a union between us is beyond anything we could ever have dreamed of or imagined on our own! And it applies to everyone, saint or sinner, you or me, now! But how?

The answer to that question brings us to the next stage of the journey to union with Christ through our own human condition. We are fortunate that out of our best biblical tradition the great saints, with the blessing of the Church, push the edges of the mystery, so that we can now even dare to speak of my personal pain being Christ's pain now. Jesus Christ, the Son of God, seated at the right hand of the Father, somehow bears my pain in His risen flesh now! Although He does not come to that pain through sin, if it is there in me it is there in Him! And Jesus wants us to know that and live from that place in our soul, in our psyche. What an incredible union!

"But" you might be thinking, "not for the likes of me." It *is* for the likes of you and me! It is! That's the whole point! But because we are not simple enough, childlike enough, about our own human condition we need help to take such a leap of faith. Once again the Spirit is lavish at this moment on the journey. Enter the Saints!

4   Beyond Biblical Roulette

*"Down through the centuries and genera-
tions it has been seen that in suffering there
is concealed a particular power that draws
a person interiorly close to Christ, a special
grace. To this grace many saints ... owe
their profound conversion.* **A result of
such a conversion is not only that the
individual discovers the salvific meaning of suffering but above all that he
becomes a completely new person. He
discovers a new dimension, as it were,
of his entire life and vocation** *... (emphasis my own.) ... Nevertheless, it often takes
time, even a long time, for this ... to begin to
be interiorly perceived. For Christ does not
answer directly and he does not answer in
the abstract this human questioning about
the meaning of suffering. Man hears Christ's
saving answer as he himself gradually
becomes a sharer in the sufferings of
Christ."*[13]

Perhaps no Christian tradition recognizes more
clearly than we in the Catholic tradition what
appalling things can happen when someone

---

13   John Paul II, *Salvifici Doloris* ("The Christian Meaning of
Human Suffering.") Par. 26.

takes a single word or notion from sacred scripture and then goes away and lives it out on their own with little biblical or communal context. This "biblical roulette" is often most tempting when we find ourselves alone in the solitude and pain of our own human condition for long periods of time, wanting "an answer" so badly we can imagine any "word" to be from God. That is not what I am referring to here. I did not receive a word "from God." I believe that Christ, The Word, simply pierced my hard heart when all was ready as He does with most of us. And it didn't happen in a vacuum. It was sprinkled with other words, other graces, other people's vision and gifts over the years. It was honed on the scriptures, the Body and Blood of Jesus and the heroism of great saints. Nevertheless, it does eventually involve the risk of taking something from the Gospel literally, which is to say, taking Jesus literally.

Indeed, as Christians, we are supposed to always be "taking Jesus literally at some level, one way or the other—we can't be Christian otherwise. And we know that the commandment to love as Jesus loved is the final measure, the primary "literal word" for us from the Gospel. But we also know that we have to live through the struggle and pain of trying to conform our own social, political, economic, psychological lives to the call of the Gospel. How we finally embrace His call to love as He loved is different for each of us, though the biblical and theological boundaries are the same.

As is often the case at certain crucial moments along the journey, the Holy Spirit gives someone to us, in the flesh or in the written word, someone who seems to have walked a path similar to our own, though far beyond us. I was singularly blessed in this regard because my guide was not a high powered evangelist or a healer, by current criteria, but seemingly a very simple woman, who really turns out to be a saint.

This is not the time or place to attempt a significant presentation of the spirituality of Catherine de Hueck Doherty whose Cause for canonization has already begun and whose many books are readily available. (www.madonnahouse.org/publications) But for my purpose here I do need to focus a bit on her special charisma and how it changed my whole sense of my own human situation and thus my personal relationship, my union with Christ.

Catherine Doherty literally believed that anything and everything she did to anyone, sinner or saint, she did to Jesus Christ personally, in the flesh. And she believed it because she took Christ literally when He said that what we do to others we do to Him. I had never met anyone like that. I had read about them. I knew they had come and gone from within my own faith tradition but I had never met one in the flesh. Nor was it clear to me at all what she was talking about until I had spent a long time "in the desert" and then had access to her personal writings a few years later.

> *"It often takes time, even a long time, for this ... to begin to be interiorly perceived. For Christ does not answer directly and he does not answer in the abstract this human questioning about the meaning of suffering. Man hears Christ's saving answer as he himself gradually becomes a sharer in the sufferings of Christ."*[14]

But as I went deeper into Catherine's life, especially through her writings, I realized that not only did she believe that anything and everything she did to anyone, sinner or saint, she did to Jesus Christ but, her pain was His pain and His pain was hers, and thus theirs! That is how clearly Catherine saw into the depths of the Incarnation and her own personal union with Christ *now*. She was indeed aware that Jesus was her personal saviour and that she was called by Him to witness that to the whole world. But far beyond that she had a truly mystical sense that what happened to her now happened to Christ

---

14   John Paul II, Ibid.

now because we are one! Her loneliness was His loneliness and if she came to anyone in their loneliness she came to Christ in His. By assuaging them, quenching their loneliness, she assuaged His. And then He assuaged hers.

Nor she did not stop there. Soon, in the late hours of the night, she would awaken and discover in her own flesh the pain of some distant soul and because of her union in Christ she could "walk" with that soul and assuage their pain without moving an inch in time. And by walking with them she walked with Christ.

And here we reach the peak of the mountain, the reason for the whole journey, the cause of our joy as Pope John Paul II says:

> *"In contemplating Christ's face, we confront the most paradoxical aspect of his mystery, as it emerges in his last hour, on the cross ... the paradoxical blending of bliss and pain ... The mystery within the mystery, before which we cannot but prostrate ourselves in adoration ... "* [15]

Devotional romanticism? Not for Catherine! For her this is the normal fruit of a life-long fidelity to the Word of God, sacred scripture, and

---

15   John Paul II, *Novo Millennio Ineunte*. (The Beginning of the New Millenium.) Par. 25.

a heroic obedience to the Gospel-Sacramental community of the Church. And it is there, in the Church, that the charisma of the saints meld with the Spirit and together open up the very Gospel Itself with new vision and hope based fundamentally on a real and particular union with Jesus Christ now, God in the flesh.

> "*Down through the centuries and generations it has been seen that in suffering there is concealed a particular power that draws a person interiorly close to Christ, a special grace. To this grace many saints ... owe their profound conversion. A result of such a conversion is not only that the individual discovers the salvific meaning of suffering but above all that he becomes a completely new person. He discovers a new dimension, as it were, of his entire life and vocation ...*"[16]

I knew, by some Faith instinct, that what Catherine Doherty was living and proclaiming was holy because once again I too began to do what all Christians should be doing naturally all the time: namely to look for those "literal" connections in our own personal lives now, with *Christ* now. And what I found to be so fascinating at that particular moment on the journey was

---

16   John Paul II, *Salvifici Doloris*, op.cit.

how this vision of union with Christ opened me up again to the vast wealth of spiritual wisdom and experience from within my own Catholic tradition, especially the lives of the saints, and ultimately to sacred scriptures.

I have neither the time nor the expertise to attempt an in-depth presentation of the countless ways in which the Spirit has taught the Church and led individuals in the Church into this particular spirituality of union with Christ through the human condition. I only point out a few of the things by which the Spirit has also guided me along the way.

One of the first sources I went back to while in the solitude was a one-time favourite of mine, *The Mysteries of Christianity*, by Msgr. Matthias Scheeben—1835-1888. (I have heard him referred to as "the von Balthasar of the 19th century.")

> *"The entire race likewise becomes the body and flesh of the Word, not in a purely moral sense, but as truly and really as the union of the race with the humanity of Christ, and the union of this humanity with the divine person are true and real ... And in general it is not only we who suffer, but Christ suffers in us, with sufferings that resemble those He sustained in His own humanity ...*

Christ's lot, His sufferings and activities, are ours, on account of our union with Him."[17]

Then I rediscovered some of the great writers of my own era who wrote about this incredible union with Christ: there was Fr. Gerald Vann, OP, whom I have already quoted, but I also returned to another old favorite, Paul de Jaegher, SJ, and his classic, *One With Jesus.* Fr. de Jaegher writes that it is not a question of Christ descending to our own level to live our life within us, but *"that he may live his own life in us."*[18] This is no mere imitation of Christ as if the soul puts on Christ's features but rather we allow *"Christ to develop and reproduce himself"*[19] in us.

I wandered back into some of the life-giving encyclicals about Christ and our baptismal union with Him: *Miserentissimus Redemptor,* "Our Most Merciful Redeemer," by Pius XI, (1928) and *Mystici Corporis Christi,* "The Mystical Body of Christ," by Pius XII, (1947.) I re-read, *Redemptor Hominis,* "The Redeemer of Man" and *Salvifici Doloris,* "The Power of Salvific Suffering," both by Pope John Paul II.

And of course I walked quietly through the scriptures again with my heart open to any

---

17   Matthias Scheeben, *The Mysteries of Christianity.* B. Herder Book Co., St. Louis, Missouri, 1946. Chapter XIV. pgs. 368,371.
18   Paul de Jaegher, *S.J., One With Jesus.* Newman Press, Westminster, Maryland, 1958. Chapter II, pg. 14. Chapter IV, pg. 32.
19   Ibid.

images of this mysterious and holy union with Christ in our flesh. But even though there were many memorable passages, it was St. Paul who kept me in biblical reality when he reminded me that we embrace in our own body all that still has to be undergone by Christ for the sake of his body, the church (Col 1:24), so that carrying in our body the death of Jesus, the life of Jesus will be visible in our flesh (2 Cor 4:10-11). With that biblical rock in place, then my favorite words of St. Paul's stood out in bold print, namely, that we live, not ourselves, but Christ lives in us (Gal 2:19-20) so we can grow into union with him through a death like his and be united with him in his resurrection (Rom 6:5).

Quite unexpectedly, I discovered one of the most unusual and profound books on this whole topic that I think I have ever read. It is by a French Jesuit, Francois Varillon, who died in the late 1970's. It is titled, *The Humility And Suffering of God.*[20] I recommend it with mindful caution because even though the book has an Imprimatur, Fr. Varillon, a very prayerful theologian and astute professor of philosophy and literature, is pushing the edges of the mystery of Christ's humanity *vis à vis* God The Father and Holy Spirit beyond what many are accustomed to.

---

20   Francois Varillon, *The Humility And Suffering of God.* Alba House, New York, 1983. Chapter 4, page 129.

But as we all might, Varillon well-imagines that if the suffering of God's creatures does not "move God" then what of the sufferings of the One the Father sent, the Son made man, who suffered in such agony that his sweat turned to blood. Fr. Varillon wonders if we can possibly imagine God, like some Supreme Being, merely looking on the Son from eternal "bliss", and did not "shiver" at His own Son's agony?

Renewed by such words of wisdom and hope it did not take me long to recall once again how the fullness of the Gospel is given new flesh through the lives of our saints, and that the Holy Spirit does indeed "reveal" aspects of the mystery of the Incarnation and facets of the human-divine personality of the Son of God that are not always immediately present to us, and gives them to us at a time when our faith is in danger from many sides. And so, when I saw the Gospel unfold into the most practical, life-giving, relationship with Christ and everyone else whom Catherine Doherty met in the flesh or in the spirit, and when I saw the mystery of "pain and bliss" become one in her own flesh, I was ... I was dumbfounded again. It was so simple: for her, everything was about Christ. Literally! Everything! Eventually even her tears!

> *"You must never forget ... that when I weep,*
> *Christ weeps, because Christ is in me.*

*When my tears mingle with those of Christ,
then his holiness washes me, not mine ... I
believe in faith that they are from God, that
I am crying with him because he cares for
me and cries with me ... Something happened in the world that made God cry and
he invited me to cry. Or perhaps I cried and
invited him to cry ... "*[21]

Really? Well, one night in the solitude when I
was weeping again, even though my tears were
mostly for my own sins, I said to myself, "What
if Catherine is right? What if these are not just
my tears but the tears of Christ? What if these
are not my tears but those of someone else and
Christ is inviting me to weep with them, with
him? What if? What if it is literally true to say
that anything I suffer, anything, Christ also suffers in some very real, mystical-body fashion,
personally, now? What if it is literally true to say
that there is no suffering in the world that Christ
does not also suffer personally in some way,
now? What if it is literally true that our whole
lives are a preparation undertaken by Christ at
our Baptism to bring us into the fullness of His
Incarnation through our own human condition
now? What if?

---

[21]   Catherine Doherty, *Poustinia*. Madonna House Publications.
Combermere, Ontario, Canada, 1993. Chapter 9. "Confrontation
with Evil and Martyrdom." Pgs. 118, 119.

Do you hear the intellectual wheels turning, pushing away from what it imagines to be irrational? Do you hear the theological wheels grinding out their cry for caution lest you get lost in some devotional neurosis? Do you hear the social, political wheels screeching to a halt, shouting out their typical historical warning "that kind of religious mumbo-jumbo has never changed anything?" Do you hear your poor Psyche crying out louder than all the rest, "that's crazy!"?

Well, what if: " ... *what happens between birth and death is message, challenge, test, succor—is all from his hands. It is not meant to be learned theoretically, but personally experienced and assimilated..and until a man makes this transposition he will have no peace*" ? [22]

What if: " ... *you are one with Jesus ... All that is his is yours ... his breath in your breath, his heart in your heart, all the faculties of his soul in the faculties of your soul ... you have one breath with him, one soul, one life, one will, one mind, one heart ... He desires that whatever is in him may live and rule in you ... *"[23]

What if our personal Christian life is all about Christ in His humanity and our union with His

---

22 Guardini, op.cit.
23 Eudes, op.cit.

as we are now?   And what if my particular human condition, regardless of how I got here, is the primary source of that union, now and that the " *... result ... is not only that the individual discovers the salvific meaning of suffering but above all that he becomes a completely new person. He discovers a new dimension, as it were, of his entire life and vocation ...* "?[24]

Yes! **What if?**

---

24   John Paul II, *Salvifici Doloris*, op.cit.

5   Heart to Heart

In an article on the Catholic practice of devotion to Christ under the image of His Sacred Heart, Fr. John McDade, SJ, writes: *"Karl Barth attacks the Catholic devotion to the Sacred Heart as a form of 'Jesus-worship' and 'a deification of the creature'. It is an instance [of a] ... doctrine or practice which aims at making the human nature, the historical and psychological manifestation of Jesus as such, its object ... in the Heart of Jesus cult ... it is blatantly a matter of finding a generally illuminating access to Jesus Christ which evades the divinity of the Word ... by direct glorification of Christ's humanity [and] as such the divine Word is evaded and camouflaged."*

Fr. McDade continues, *"[but] the Catholic tradition [on the other hand is] so much at home with the presence of the Word among us that it builds cribs to celebrate his birth, paints crucifixes to remember his death and explicitly venerates images of his saints; it is so struck by redemptive love—that, after all, is what the Sacred Heart devotion represents—that its spontaneous practice is to light candles before a statue of the Sacred Heart as a sign that Christ's light is received by us. This intimate sense of being 'at home' in the visible and saving presence of the Word always accompanies the practice of devotions in Catholic popular culture. And this sensibility, avail-*

able to all whatever their level of education, flows from a different reading of the Incarnation ... You may think yourself out of Christian faith, the devotion seems to be saying, but you cannot think yourself out of Christ's love for you because the more you reject him, the more you are loved by him. In his death, he has already borne the wounds of human brutality, turning those wounds into channels of forgiveness."[25]

When I was a child it was quite normal for me to fancy the heart of Jesus—to come to God as someone who "had a heart!" Perhaps the music surrounding that devotion was exceedingly sentimental and the art sometimes gaudy, to say the least, but there was something extraordinary about the fact that Jesus Himself, through many apparitions, was trying to make known to us a very unique affection, indeed union, between His heart, His humanity, and our own. The Lord was not trying to "camouflage or evade His divinity" (Mr. Barth) but to show us that our humanity was "divine" and newly "sacred" in Him through Baptism, and that such a relationship was so new it could only be understood "Heart to heart!"

I didn't have all those fancy words about the Sacred Heart as a child—when you are a little

25 "Devotion to the Sacred Heart." John McDade SJ *The Way Supplement,* 100, *Popular Devotions* (Spring. 2001), 22-29.

child the things of the Kingdom are simple indeed! For a child, yes. But by 1980, when I was almost 50, I had long-since lost a need for or desire for a relationship with Christ as the Sacred Heart of Jesus. I didn't object to the devotion or its place in Catholic liturgical life but it simply was no longer appealing to me. I knew well that with the exception of our relationship to Christ sacramentally, especially in Eucharist and the Blessed Sacrament, perhaps no other mode of relationship had as much place or influence in the annals of Catholic spirituality over the last 400 or so years than that of the Sacred Heart of Jesus, but it had not figured in my life for many decades. So it was a surprise to me that my own journey eventually ushered me back into that theology, that devotion. And I was even more surprised to learn how many great saints were led into a unique and intimate personal union with Christ through this image of His Sacred Heart. Among them are such spiritual giants as Saints Gertrude, Bernard, Bonaventure, Francis de Sales, Aloysius Gonzaga, John Eudes, Margaret Mary Alacoque and most recently, St. Faustina, to mention only a famous few.

In any case, one day as I was walking in a mall, I saw this gaudy picture of the Sacred Heart in a store window, walked right in and bought it. Just like that! And then I found myself often sitting alone before this picture lit by a candle and just looking at it. It still wasn't "my cup of tea," but my curiosity was piqued and I began to look more seriously at some of the biblical and sacramental theology behind this devotion. In the end it led me back into a Catholic spirituality I had never understood and wanted no part of, namely "victim-soul."

To understand this very curious kind of union in Christ one has to realize that we, to use Fr. McDade's words, have "*a different reading of the Incarnation.*" The notion of Christ being in our human condition now, though seated at the right hand of the Father, is at the heart of our Catholic sense of baptismal union with Christ, our personal savior. But Christ was also the victim Who reconciled us to God, once and for all, and yet, over and over He reveals Himself to us as One still caught up in being victim. Indeed, not as He once was, for He is now seated at the right hand of the Father, but He is victim now in a mystical fashion. Meaning? It is real but beyond our human concepts! It is into this mystical mode that He invites us to know Him now as God Who truly has a heart, and He looks for simple folk to join him, Heart to heart, in that mysterious, mystical union, "victims" with Him for the sins of the world, victim-souls.

I never quite understood what that meant until I read St. Augustine who, in answer to a similar quandry said: *"Give me one who loves, and he will understand ... "* [26].

When Pope John Paul II speaks of that *"conversion [wherein] the individual discovers the salvific meaning of suffering ... [and] ... hears Christ's saving answer as he himself gradually becomes a sharer in the sufferings of Christ,"* [27] he was surely speaking about some aspect of this spirituality of victim-soul.

This notion of victim-soul is at the center of our Sacred Heart spirituality. (Yes, Mr. Barth, that's about as "catholic" as you can get, and I do understand your apprehension. I had my own.) But that is not where the Sacred Heart "took me" this time on my journey. I did not return to the traditional spirituality of being a victim with Christ but went into something which seemed to unfold for me through a simple awareness of the union between us in the flesh. As I focussed on union with Christ Who truly has a Heart what I began to see was that the union happens by way of a mutual experience in Christ, namely, our

---

26 St. Augustine, *In Johannis Evangelium*, tract. XXVI, 4
27 John Paul II, *Salvifici Doloris,* op.cit.

mutual human condition; my pain is their pain is His pain. We are one in Christ! For me that was not about being a victim but about some new sense of union, which I now call "sacrificial-soul" to distinguish it from the spirituality of victim-soul. Sacrificial-soul spirituality focuses on the mystery of being one with Christ and each other, through our mutual human condition, now. And this mutual human condition now is the primary source of the personal relationship we have with Jesus through Baptism, He Who is "our personal saviour." But the emphasis is on the union and not on victim!

The first clear sense I had of this change of emphasis in my relationship with Christ, this sacrificial-soul union vs. victim-soul, was in that experience I have already shared when I "imag-ined" Him telling me that He had been the one being abused and had actually invited me to be one with Him. With time that experience and its image of union began to couple and meld with similar events in my life, one of which I shared from my relationship with Catherine Doherty about her sense of weeping with Christ. If you remember, I ended that particular chapter with a series of "what if's." It was not meant to be a hap-less spiritual exercise. I was being very literal. Because as I began to open my heart literally to such "what if's" in my own life along the way, I became more and more aware that the events of each day were really all about my personal union/relationship with Christ through our mutual human condition now. And it was a whole new adventure in Faith to find and make the connections with Him moment by moment, day by day.

I had never done that before at least not to this intensity. And it wasn't long before I realized that if I was going to keep this new sacrificial-soul focus at the center of my own faith life in the flesh, I needed a new discipline, a new ascesis, a new way to stay focussed on Christ. If I was going to focus on my everyday union with Christ in the flesh I needed to discipline myself, in the flesh, in a very particular way. But how? It had to be simple for the likes of me!

By now on the journey I knew pretty clearly I had three levels of pain that I was dealing with in my life, in my flesh, three levels of the human condition, if you will. Number one was the condition of the world, the pain of the world over which I had no immediate control. Secondly was the pain others caused me, knowingly or not, past or present. And finally the pain I caused myself and everyone else around me because of my own wounds or sins. That's a lot of life in which to stay focussed. How Lord? How? Well, one night there before my gaudy picture of the Sacred

Heart I just asked for help: "Jesus, how am I going to daily enter into this new and mysterious sacrificial-soul union?"

I don't recall any voice in answer to my question but here is how my prayer unfolded. This is how I learned to be aware of my personal union with Christ in the flesh through what is happening to me at any given time in my flesh.

What do I do first of all with the pain and suffering in the world that seeps into my consciousness, for which I am not directly responsible, but which can flood in upon me and cause such intense pain? When I see or hear or read of any suffering happening in the world which often causes a personal response from me—tears, sadness, pain, helplessness, etc.—I immediately imagine that it is first of all about Christ! What I am feeling now, in my flesh, is His pain in and through the pain of others. And in some generous, intimate way His joy is to invite me into His through theirs. It's the only way I have found by which to embrace pain on a world scale, pain which is not under my control or my immediate responsibility but is part of the human condition that I know and see, even from a distance. I can do nothing about it except in Him!

What about that pain which comes upon me through others during the day, or through past

memories of similar pain, just or unjust?   Well,
if Christ is the focus, then everything is about
Him and me and not about me and them!
Whatever happens now happens because He
wants to draw me into Himself and not teach me
how to clear up my own emotional life or inter-
personal relationship with you! That comes
later.

How does He draw me? Through my humanity
as it is now!   This is not a "what would Jesus do"
spirituality.   This is about union now in Christ
through our human condition. We must not ask,
"What would Jesus do?" but rather "Jesus, you
experienced something like this in Your life—for
different reasons than mine—so what kind of
union with You are You calling me to right now
through my humanity? What are You trying to
teach me about You and Your relationship with
Your Father right now in and through my
flesh?"

If such spirituality is to be at the center of our
emotional life, we have to let go of all those normal questions like, "why did they do that to
me?" or "how should I deal with them?" or "how
can I create my own boundaries when I am
around them?" or whatever else. No! If the focus
is Christ then sooner or later the only question
which will bring us life is: "Lord Jesus what are

You trying to show me about Your relationship to the Father through this event, in my flesh, now?" Period. If we can't put a period after that question and let all the other questions go for the time being then we need to go back into the solitude by whatever means until there are no more questions but that one: "What are You trying to teach me, now?" Because what we are really asking Christ is: "How can my heart become 'sacred,' secure in Your Heart now, in the flesh?"

Finally, what about the pain that comes entirely from within myself whether from my own sin or those ancestral wounds that still abide? This is the most difficult to put words on, to work through, to find the connection between myself and Christ, because, after all, are not most of these inner wounds and memories, as we live them out now, the result of our own personal sins? How can Christ be involved in that? Well, I don't know "theologically," but I do know that enigma was ended for me with those awesome words that night in the solitude: "*It was not you who was being abused ... It was Me.*" Period!

Now, when I am in pain of any kind caused by my own sins or some personal situation flowing from them, I go to the Sacred Heart and I say to Him, with all my flesh, "I am now everyone in the world who is in this same sin/pain/wound

that I am in right now! I am them! We are one!"
I no longer focus on the shame or guilt or sadness
brought on by my own sin. Gradually my heart
became "bigger" than my own sin or pain or
shame or guilt. Something happened which
allowed me to focus first on the union between
me and all other sinners through my sin, as I am
now. And when that sense of union with all of
them became my focus, then I began to see that
Christ was already there in *my* pain too, even
though the pain began perhaps because of my
own fault or failure; He is there in mine because
He is there in theirs. In His tremendous love for
us He has turned our pain into His! And being
one in Him we can speak to His Sacred Heart as
we are right now for those who will not go there.
The mystery is that we do so humbly, through the
pain and shame of our own sin, our own weakness, and in Christ we can do for them what they
cannot or will not do for themselves! This is the
gift we have been given through our Baptism:
sacrificial-souls, one with the Son of God, with
all of humanity.

In any case, the key has been to go directly to His
pain through my pain and then talk to Him about
them, and not *me,* even though *I* am the one who
"sinned" or who is in pain because of past sin. If
I weep now I weep for them first, before I ever
weep for myself, because *He* is weeping! It's

about Him first before it's ever about me. And then when the cry of my heart and my tears "become one with His" suddenly we are all one, saints and sinners, harlots and hermits, abused and abusers, all one in the Body of the incarnate Son of God through the Sacred Heart of Jesus, in the flesh! And it all happens in the most normal though now sacred way, namely, through, with and in our common human condition, which makes us one in the very Body of Christ.   Thus that awesome *"paradoxical blending of pain and bliss"*[28] when the Most Sacred Heart of Jesus assuages us all together even if we are millions of miles apart. This then the priesthood of the baptized!

How do we explain that? I don't know—it's hard enough to put words on it. But I know it is there at the heart of our Catholic biblical spirituality, for it is there in the Heart of Christ. And I know that in the darkness, the solitude, the desert when there are no more answers because there were no more questions, "someone" teaches us in *That Place* that our suffering and pain is no longer just about us. It is also about Christ and thus about everyone else because we are one in Christ. Perhaps in this mysterious union with Christ all of us, the weakest and strongest, the greatest and

---

28   John Paul II, *Novo Millennio Ineunte*, op. cit.

the least, discover that through our own human condition, in the flesh, it is not we who live but Christ who lives in us (Col. 2:20). Perhaps St. Paul is not talking about a union in Christ that happens when I "get holy enough" so that Christ *can* live in me, but rather that He already *does* live in me, but I am not empty and humble enough to realize it!

No wonder then that the most natural image of such a divine relationship is this image of the Sacred Heart of Jesus. He has given us this divine revelation of Himself so we can begin to understand the heights and depths of our intimate, personal union with Him "in the flesh" now! Whatever it may mean to ask, "do you know Christ as your personal savior?" we must ask ourselves yet a deeper question, namely, "how personal is your relationship with Christ, your Savior, in your life, your flesh, as you are right now?" Do we really believe how close we are to Him whose Heart is totally open to our human condition as it is right now?

Jesus prophesied that the world would one day look upon him whom they have pierced, and taught us that if we do not fear that vision of our own sins, then when he is lifted up from the earth He would draw us to himself (Jn 19:37 and Jn 12:32). Why the Sacred Heart? **Because our**

God is all heart!   And we will know that in our own heart when we realize how much He has embraced us, in the flesh, from the moment of our conception, and how He has personally been drawing us to Himself through our own human condition from that moment until now.   Quietly, humbly, from our conception to last breath, Christ cries out to all of us, no matter what our own human situation: *"Come to me, all you who labor and are burdened, and I will give you rest. Take my yoke upon you and learn from me, for I am meek and humble of heart."* (Mt 11:28-30)   And He Himself tells us in all those wonderful apparitions it grieves Him that we will not set forth now, as we are, on the journey into His Sacred Heart and let Him take us to where we should be!

6 When it Comes to Evil ...

> " ... *Our Lord Jesus Christ gave a sign to*
> *His servants who fear Him, that they*
> *might cast out devils ... a sign to His ser-*
> *vants who fear Him, that they might*
> *vanquish their enemies. The sign is the*
> *saving name of Our Lord Jesus Christ ...*
> *blessed is the one who ... cleaves with his*
> *heart and mind to the saving name of our*
> *Lord Jesus Christ ... "*

Taken from "*Psalmody to the Lord Jesus Christ*" from the Coptic
Liturgy.

I wrote the prologue to this book sometime in
the mid 70's. It is not a literary device; it was
really how I experienced my life and faith in a
nutshell, 25 words or less! It began as a kind of
personal soul-response to all that tedious and
ofttimes boring journal mode we were in at the
time: everyone and their dog felt obliged to journal their every thought, word and deed as if they
had finally, almost single-handed, discovered the
real truth about everything, and were thus
obliged to write it down and share it with the
whole world—if not a book then on a banner or
a button!

Perhaps this was a noble effort and one that
brought new hope for others, but it was a mode

that did not attract me, because two very important things were often missing, things which I
had almost lost myself.

The first of these was the idea that the New
Commandment is the final measure of the
Christian life. It is not the issues, secular or
ecclesiastical, not whether one managed to avoid
appearing on the long list of public sins to which
it seemed everyone else belonged but themselves. It is not being politically correct, and
surely not "luv." The daily and final measure of
the Christian life is the New Commandment, the
Love of Jesus Christ. Secondly what was often
missing for me in the contemporary journal
mode is what people did with the reality of Evil,
how they approached it, explained it, responded
to it. By then, for many, Evil was a normal ying
and yang, up and down, light and dark, a kind
of complement to the mystery of matter and life.
But it was not about an objective Person outside
the Self.

Coupled with all of that confusion it seemed to
many of us that the pastoral Church, like the
State, was locked in on its own survival and
could not open up to any new and significant
life-giving call of the Gospel which the world
was crying out for with its very blood. In my
own denial and desperation I became one of
those self-righteous accusers pointing out every-

body else's failures except my own!   And when my own hallowed life began to unravel, I discovered that when all the political pomp and social circumstance was over I too was locked into spiritual, political, psychological survival at all costs. I was a bourgeois-believer with no room in my life anymore for "what if."   And I discovered, not too late, thank God, that a faith-life without "what if" spells death, and I was dying.

It is not unusual that when the light of Faith begins to die out we often meet the Evil One before the Darkness sets in.   I sure as Hell did! And it was the best thing that ever happened to me, for once you know that Evil is a Person there is no doubt that both Life and Faith are "personal"—very Personal!

Once again, enters: Catherine Doherty.   As I already said, in the late 60's, as part of my own journey, I found myself in a log cabin back in the bush of Canada, living a new and strange spirituality which she had brought to North America from her Russian roots, called "Poustinia". (By 1975 she would write a book by the same title.) Let me hazard to simplify and say that poustinia, which means "desert" in Russian, is all the fullness of what we mean by "hermitage" from within Western tradition with a significant Eastern trait: the door to the "poustinia" is always open to the needs of the community. In other words though perhaps it first looks very much like hermitage, life in poustinia is formed and modified by a life in community according to its needs and mandate.

In those days we who lived in poustinia according to Catherine's vision spent three days alone in the physical cabin and four days living and working in the family. At that time I could not pray. I could not read the scriptures. And I did not want anything to do with spiritual or political issues. And as priest I had nothing to say or offer anyone because I could barely manage myself. So, what would I do for three days alone in the Canadian Bush?

Well, I discovered three things which were still alive in my own heart: I still enjoyed reading the lives of the saints who had always attracted me, I still had a unexplainable love for the Eucharist and so I offered Mass everyday alone, and I had also recently succumbed to the new fad of the 60's, namely the Jesus Prayer. This prayer was made popular for most of us in the 1961 novel "*Franny and Zooey*," by J.D. Salinger wherein he focussed on the classic tradition of that holy prayer as found in "*The Way of a Pilgrim*" and the "*Philokalia.*"

I paid no particular attention to the traditional "technique" of The Jesus Prayer, I simply voiced it as I breathed in and out—I couldn't pray but I could breathe! I didn't even know at the time that this way of saying the prayer was part of any monastic technique. I only knew that saying and hearing it brought me hope at a time when there was little or none for me. And so, for hours on end I would kneel or sit or lie down, breathing in "Lord Jesus Christ, Son of the Living God, be merciful to me, a sinner," and breathing out "Lord Jesus Christ, Son of the Living God, be merciful to me, a sinner." In and out, over and over until all I was breathing was the single word—Jesus. When that Word was germaine to my soul and psyche again, I had my first personal encounter with the Person of Evil.

By that time in my life, as I have already hinted, I too had begun to imagine that Good and Evil were more akin to light and darkness, up and down, and all those yings and yangs found in creation, but nothing real, certainly nothing personal. So then, one night while I was praying in the poustinia, how did something that is not real, not personal, pick me up, throw me around the room and then out the door into the darkness outside? No, this was not light and dark, up and down, ying and yang. This was person-to-person. And I knew it just as clearly as I knew that I was personally breathing the personal name of the Son of God when it all began. But how could the Evil One do that if I was under the mantle of Christ's own name?

Well, that's a major lesson on the journey. By Baptism we are freed from the Evil One's power as we travel but we are not freed from the Evil One's actions, effects or signs. And you best be aware of how to confront them: not on your own, for you have no power there, but by the power given to the Church "in the Name of Jesus."

It was evermore significant that this all happened to me in a place where other priests were available, even out in the Bush at midnight, to pray over me, to bless me and protect me. But when I finally realized that I had the Name of Jesus on my lips *as the Evil One struck* it became the most powerful word in the whole language of faith for me, even if all of Hell was mocking and half of my eternity had gone by.

As if that were not enough: often over the years my soul was very much in danger as I moved back and forth between the sacred and the profane, back and forth between sin and sanctity, between God and the Evil One. And then somewhere along the journey I realized that I was saying the Name of Jesus even as I sinned, be it anger, sloth, gluttony, power, self-righteousness, greed, lust. Because when I breathed He was there and I couldn't stop breathing! At times I was certain that He would come and strike me dead for such blasphemy. Little did I know! The name of Jesus had become so much a part of me I could not *not* say it, no matter what! Yes, it takes more than saying, "Lord, Lord" (Jesus, Jesus) to enter the kingdom of heaven, but, now I know it is enough to keep me out of Hell! After that, Jesus can do anything!

Cheap Grace? Maybe. All I know is that when I look back now to the time before that in my life when I was so secure, such a "perfect" Christian, Grace seems to have been much cheaper, even trashy, than compared to now. Then I prayed as if I was doing something great and holy for God, all toward my own eternal salvation, of course. Now I pray out of affection and admiration for Who Christ is and who we are in Him, saints or sinners, whores or hermits. The rest is God's business.

And when it comes to Evil?

> " ... *The Lord Jesus Christ gave a sign to His servants who fear Him, that they might cast out devils ... a sign to His servants who fear Him, that they might vanquish their enemies. The sign is the saving name of Our Lord Jesus Christ ... blessed is the one who ... cleaves with his heart and mind to the saving name of our Lord Jesus Christ ... "*[28]

Jesus! Jesus! Jesus!

---

28 Coptic Liturgy, Ibid.

7   The Priesthood of the Baptized

"Suffering and the consecration it demands, cannot be understood perfectly outside the context of baptism.   For baptism, in giving us our identity, gives us a divine vocation to find ourselves in Christ. It gives us our identity in Christ. But both the grace and the character of baptism give our soul a spiritual conformity to Christ in his suffering. For baptism is the application to our souls of the Passion of Christ.

Baptism also more clearly distinguishes us ... especially from one another. For it gives us our personal, incommunicable vocation to reproduce in our own lives the life and sufferings and charity of Christ in a way unknown to anyone else who has ever lived under the sun. When I see my trials ... as the sacramental gift of Christ's love, given to me by God the Father along with my identity and my very name, then I can consecrate them and myself with them to God. For then I realize that my suffering is not my own. It is the Passion of Christ, stretching out it tendrils into my life in order to bear rich clusters of grapes, making my soul dizzy with the wine of Christ's love and

> *pouring that wine as strong as fire upon the whole world."*[29]

I had never thought of myself as a great lover. Not only did I not understand love but I felt as if I didn't receive much of it along the way. Care and compassion? Yes. Love? No. But more than that I was subordinate to whatever social distortion, emotional poverty or moral sickness surrounded the notion of love in that piece of life given to me beginning in 1931. The fact that my faith-family, the Catholic church, had an incredible chronicle of the best of the spirituality of love, did attract my attention in my early years as I began to yearn for a monastic vocation. But the ultimate satisfaction of that desire, the desire of becoming priest, did not heal the deeper wounds which made authentic love somewhat insufferable for me if not impossible. (Quite a dilemma for someone whose very Faith is based and built on a commandment by God to love as God loves!) Looking back I realize now it was not so much that I did not know how to love or had not been loved myself; it was rather that I had ceased to believe the witness of what Christian Love is and I could not believe again until something else happened to my heart.

---

29   Thomas Merton, *No Man is an Island.* Harcourt, Bruce & Co. New York. 1955. Chapter 5, pgs. 82, 83.

Love is simple because God is Love and God is Simplicity itself. So when we Christians complicate Love we give birth to all sorts of social, emotional, moral, loveless bastards: my needs, my feelings, my wants, my life, my love. All of these are rightfully there on the edges of Love but if they become central then Love dies and so do lovers. I did. Yet how eccentric of God to bring us back to Love by way of our own broken humanity in Christ, who was like us in all things except sin (Heb. 4: 15) rather than by extraordinary mystical experiences as we so often would prefer. And we discover the effects of this Love hidden in the "divine" effects of the great sacrament of our Baptism.

Whatever else happens in Christian Baptism, for certain through it God's Love is set to grow and gracefully sanctify each individual personally from that moment until the End. The enigma is that this Love is meant to mature through our own personal life history, in the flesh, so that we can finally become fully conscious of this singular union with Christ in His humanity where we learn what Love is and how to Love!

To this point the journey seems too long and difficult for us mortals, but that is so because we are preparing to enter into a vision of Love that is so astounding we must come to it very slowly. And we cannot come to it unless we go down to *That*

Place where we discover Christ deep in the human condition of our everyday lives, where we are one with others in their pain and suffering as we are urged on by the witness of our saints and all holy people. There we discover the deepest connection we can possibly have on this earth with Christ through the human condition.

Now our thirst can be assuaged through His, because He wants to take us with Him into the heart of that Love. But such Love is shrouded in His Priesthood and thus, for us, in the Priesthood of our Baptism. And it is in this "priesthood" that the fullest human dimension of Love is revealed and made possible to us! *"For baptism, in giving us our identity, gives us a divine vocation to find ourselves in Christ."*[30] This priestly character of the mystery is given to all the Baptized, ordained or not. It is not a ritual gift but it is a gift of a new order, a new way of being one with Christ which changes all our relationships, even with our own self.

There is, of course, only one Priesthood, that of Jesus Christ, but what Christ "does" as Priest has been apportioned out in different ways because it is a particular way of God loving "in the flesh" which has been revealed to us—there is no other

---

30 Merton, Ibid.

way we could possibly know this pattern of Love!

We believe that the greatest witness of this kind of Love was Christ as He died on the Cross. However true that is, it certainly scared me off from Love. Not only could I not imagine loving that way but I was in such great pain myself that the thought of more pain as a sign of love felt like suicide to me and would have been if I had not eventually come to understand and embrace my own human condition in the light of Christ's. That was the only way I could fathom why my own life had unfolded, or unravelled, as it had; it was this which made it possible for me to once again believe and embrace how each of us are one in Christ's Love, that what I do to you, the good, the bad and the ugly, I do to Him and to myself.

When that mutual caring-for and compassion-with in Christ, became "normal" for me again, another dimension of the mystery of Love could open up. For that I didn't need to know how to Love, all I had to do was embrace it at the moment when all Love seemed utterly and eternally impossible. And it happened during another one of those solitude times when my Psyche was cracked open so wide I couldn't close it. I felt as if I were dying. I began to "descend." It was not particularly frightening at first but as it progressed I realized it would end in eternal nothingness. There were no movies of my past. No voices of judgement. No condemnation. There was nothing but going down and down and down.

When I was almost totally disconnected from Reality as I had known it, in utter hopelessness and in a new kind of agony, I "heard": **"There is only mercy Here! But you must ask Me for It."** There were other "voices" too: *"It's too late for such religious mumbo-jumbo."* The voices continued: *"Ask me for my mercy." "It's too late." "Ask." "It's too late."* How long that battle lasted I don't know but it was more painful than anything I had ever known before.

Finally, not out of fear but out of some new and deep truth I simply began to say, "Jesus. Jesus. Jesus." And then, just as suddenly as it had all begun, it stopped. I shot up out of *That Place,* back into consciousness, and in that moment I knew what Love was, because I knew in my flesh, in my soul, in my psyche, what Christ does for every single human being.

My journey that night was His journey between His death and resurrection and now—to Hell and back! He was inviting me into His journey to teach me and show me what Love is! Our going there together purified my whole personal history with all its unhealed memories and ancestral wounds. It did not take the memories and wounds away but it took the sting away, the poison, the authority of the lie—by the power of new Love. No, it did not take them away, but now they were the tools of joining Christ in the flesh to go anywhere with Him for others. And what makes this Love so new, so powerful is that He does not embrace our human condition for us or with us.

As Priest in the flesh he does so *as* us. *As* us!? That is beyond our mediocre sense of victim or sacrifice or holocaust, even beyond our very sense of Love itself. This new creation of doing something *as* us rather than *for* us or *with* us, is one of the primary implications of his Priesthood and why it is so interwoven with the revelation of Love. This Priesthood is a new capacity created by God which makes it possible, even for the baptized, in Christ, to suffer as the other and not merely for them or with them.

This is the fullness of the Christian mystery of victim, of sacrifice, of holocaust and finally of Eucharistic Love—to be able to do something *as* the other and not just with them or for them. This is what makes the Love of Christ so powerful and different, unlike anything else in Creation. It gives the final meaning to Love: to *become* the other so that the other is free from what could destroy them! This is Love beyond anything we have ever imagined and this Love is what makes Jesus the Priest. In his love for us he does not stand before His Father with us or for us. *He stands there as us!*

Christ "bears our deeds" in His flesh and in His flesh cries out for us to the Father in our human condition as it is right now! Whatever state we are in at any given time, Christ embraces in His own Body, now, and stands before the Father as us in that state. And because the Father sees Him and Loves Him as His Son, the Father responds to us in that same fashion and not according to our deeds. This is the revelation of Divine Love! This is the power of the Priesthood of Jesus Christ now present in some way in all of the baptised. "*For Baptism gives us our personal, incommunicable vocation to reproduce in our own lives the life and sufferings and charity of Christ in a way unknown to anyone else who has ever lived under the sun.*" [31]

We approach the fullness of our union in Christ on earth when we begin to realize that in Christ we too *are* those who are like us in our pain right now. And in Christ we can cry out *as* them before the Father, right now, as we are! Not *for* them—that's caring. Not *with* them—that's compassion. But *as* them. That's Love.

---

31 Merton, Ibid.

And the fullest expression and experience of this love is in the Eucharist, when the ordained priest brings all of that "humanity" to the paten and cup, to the bread and wine, and Christ Himself re-creates it all into His very own sacrificial and risen Body and Blood!   It is here that our own life history with all its burdens and suffering is now fully revealed in the mystery of Christ's own Priesthood. And now, as one who is baptized, I have been given the power to embrace my human condition not out of emotional guilt or zealous neuroses but out of Love: I can *be* you in Christ before the Father, cry out *as* you, for mercy, for hope, for light, for salvation.

The Father hears me, not because I am praying, not because I am holy, but because I am one with Christ Who is one with you and me through the mystery of our union with him in the flesh, in his body, through our own human condition. *"When I see my trials . . as the sacramental gift of Christ's love, given to me by God the Father along with my identity and my very name, then I can consecrate them and myself with them to God. For then I realize that my suffering is not my own. It is the passion of Christ, strecthing out its tendrils into my life ... "* [32] When I know this then I know what it means to pray always.

---

32   Merton, Ibid.

This embrace of our human condition without undue worry or concern for our own self, our own future, in Time or Eternity, is the essence of Love. And the union with Christ through it is the source of all joy. It is not a Love we humans take to naturally, on our own. It is revealed, and is at the heart of Christ's Priesthood and our own participation in it through Baptism. But especially at the Eucharistic Sacrifice can the baptised come to see most clearly the mystery of our own human condition and the new joy which comes as we realize more and more that we are actually, really one in Jesus Christ, Priest. Nothing that happens to us is wasted; it is all "bread and wine" through which we become more and more one with Christ the Priest who takes us to His Father as we join Him through our own humanity as it is right now!

In Baptism we have all have been "loved to death" from the very beginning of our lives even if we didn't realize it because it is " ... *the Passion of Christ, stretching out it tendrils into my life in order to bear rich clusters of grapes, making my soul dizzy with the wine of Christ's love and pouring that wine as strong as fire upon the whole world.*"[33]

---

33   Merton, Ibid.

8   Mystery — The Language of Love

"After this I had a vision … a throne was there in heaven, and on the throne sat one whose appearance sparkled like jasper … around the throne was a halo as brilliant as an emerald … from the throne came flashes of lightning … and peals of thunder.   In front of the throne was … a sea of glass like crystal … and around the throne, there were four living creatures. … day and night they do not stop exclaiming: 'Holy, holy, holy is the Lord God almighty, who was, and who is, and who is to come'." (Rv 4: 1, 2, 3, 5, 6, 8)

I said that I was not much of a lover!   It might have been more on the mark to say that I didn't have much of a language of Love, and primarily so because I had gradually lost the language of mystery.   If there is anything in my pastoral life that I deeply regret, especially between 1960 and 1980, it is how easily I was enmeshed in the cunning snare of thinking we could make Faith more relevant by denuding it of its mystery. How well I see now that without mystery there is no language of Love in the Christian Faith, and without the language of Love faith dies an innocuous death much like meditation died when it became a transcendental technique for relaxation taught at the local YWCA! But if mystery takes its place again at the center of Faith it reveals a language of Love by which we can see into the very heart of the Incarnation and thus into the depths of our own personal union in Christ. There is probably no scripture more apt as the language of mystery than the Book of Revelation, the Apocalypse, but I never imagined that it is also a sophisticated language of Love.

For a very long time the Book of Revelation was the one book in all of the New Testament that I did not feel drawn to or nourished by. I was well acquainted with and nourished by certain passages from it because of their place in our own Catholic liturgical life, especially one of my favorites about the woman dressed in the sun, standing on the moon with the stars around her head. In our Catholic biblical tradition we take that to also imply Mary, the mother of Christ, the Mother of God. But I was turned off to most of the book because of what I perceived to be a somewhat macabre "apocalypse-now" twist which I found in so much of the contemporary evangelical witness. If I had remained steadfast to my own Catholic biblical roots I could have avoided that aloofness because ours is indeed a very provident approach which does not allow the truly apocalyptic vein to be eclipsed by mere "signs of the times." The heart of the Book of

Revelation, for us, is the revelation of the divine depths of Christ's life, death and resurrection, of His total and ultimate victory. Alleluia! I had lost that sense. It was in the desert that this book reawakened in me that mystery and its consequent language of Love which is so particular to this "in-the-flesh" relationship we have with the Risen Lord, and without which Faith dies.

By this time in the desert, I was a wee bit on the zany side because of the acute silence, and decided to read out loud from the bible just to keep from going over the edge. I had already silently read everything in the bible but the Book of Revelation. So I decided to have a little biblical stage-show right there in the desert and the script would be the Book of Revelation—I would have my own "apocalypse-now" by reading this mysterious book out loud! So there I was, the star of the show, dressed with the hot sun, standing on a huge bolder the size of half a city block in the middle of the Sinai desert, acting out, bellowing out the entire book of Revelation, line by line, chapter by chapter.

It was standing room only for the local wild animals and critters who must have been wondering who this alien was and where he had parked his UFO. But I just kept reciting the whole book out loud with all the apocalyptic drama, putting my own flesh on the words and taking them to heart without trying to figure out the "signs of the times." It was quite delightful. So, I did it again the next day and the next day. And then I stopped somewhere in the middle of a line, looked out over the bleak Sinai desert, up at the dazzling sky, back down to the book in hand, and realized that for three days I had been looking into the very heart of the Incarnation by way of a whole new language. And, I understood every word even though I could not have explained them to anyone else then and cannot even to this day when I read them.

To this day, whenever I am bereft of hope, caught in my depression or no longer able to trust Love, I can read aloud from this holy book and all is well. Once again the mystery comes forth in the awesome language of apocalyptic Love, the *"One like the Son of Man"* doing things in our flesh we could never have dreamed of. And, we are somehow right there with Him! I can't explain it. It's like breathing His Name: I just know that it **is**. Just as I know, in my heart, that the Spirit had led me back into the most profound level of the mystery of the Incarnation which is itself the fullness of the language of Love.

And for me now, without this book, my sense of Love would be acutely deficient. To me the Book of Revelation intimates in graphic language what was really happening all along in the life of

Christ from conception, through birth and death, resurrection and now until the end of time. Even as a child in the womb, He was the Alpha and the Omega, the beginning and the end (Rev 21:6), so that from the first moment of the Incarnation Christ had already begun to cast the devil into the pool of fire for ever and ever (Rev 20:10). And, even now, we on earth can join the huge crowds impossible to number standing around the throne, and shout with them that victory comes from our God who is seated on the throne, and from the Lamb. *"Blessing and glory, wisdom and thanksgiving, honor, power and might be to our God forever and ever. Amen." (Rev 7:10)*

No, the Book of Revelation is not principally a book about the "signs of the times" but about Him who is as immense as all Time and yet robed in our flesh, a mystery so great we can only grasp it by signs and symbols.   In our midst there is no mystery greater than God become Man, and, perhaps no scripture more intense with the language of that mystery than this book of Revelation.   And yet this mysterious language is also a language of Love because it is the language of union between the Incarnate Son of God and we mortals who, in Baptism, are now one with Him "in the flesh!"   Through this language we can finally come to realize that *"the chain of acts and events that runs from our first hour*

through our last..[is indeed] all from his hands.[34]
Through it we are drawn into the heart of the
mystery where " ... *his breath [is] in our breath, his
heart in our heart, all the faculties of his soul in the
faculties of our soul ... we have one breath with him,
one soul, one life, one will, one mind, one heart ... He
desires that whatever is in him may live and rule in
us ... "*[35]

Nothing reveals the depths of the Incarnation
like this holy book does and thus nothing reveals
the depths of our union with Christ like it does.
The Book of Revelation opens the mystery up to
us, lifts the veil so we can see Time and Eternity,
Heaven and Hell, the Divine and Human, in one
sweep, and giving us but a hint of the joy that
should be ours even now.

For the Christian journey inward is ultimately
meant to be a journey into joy. The joy is not
ours as if we have to manufacture it by our own
emotions. The joy is the unfathomable gladness
which Christ knows now as He continues to take
upon Himself the ache and the delight of our
own human condition: He then shares His joy
with us! Such joy can only blossom and bloom
in us when we embrace fully the union between
Him and us, when we "get the connection." And
one of the reasons we sometimes do not get the

---

34 Guardini, *op.cit*
35 Eudes, *op.cit*

connection is because we have lost the language of mystery, which is, in fact the language of Love —meant to lead us into boundless joy even now, here on earth.

Such joy is not a change in our personal human condition or some new miraculous power over our feelings and emotions and tendencies—that and more is meant to come to us in a very normal and holy fashion—but this joy is first and foremost that of knowing in our own flesh, even as we are now, that we are one with Christ in each other and his apocalyptic victory is ours. That is the joy! We have reached that moment on the journey when the meaning of our whole life, all its warts and wonders, be we saints or sinners, has been revealed to us: we are one with Christ Jesus in a way we never could have imagined, wonderfully alive and now *"lost in God"* —and now our joy is complete.

9   The Prayer of Becoming

" ... *prayer is born when the mystery of God
and the mystery of man meet. This power
and this glory are given to us that we might
daily become more like Christ, that we daily
become the way to the Father. This power
and glory are given to us so that we might
realize we are brothers and sisters of Christ,
and that we, too, have been sent to do the
will of the Father and, thus, to lead all to
him. The power and the mystery entrusted
to us is given that we might ultimately say,
'It is no longer I who live, but Christ who
lives in me' (Gal 2:20 RSV). That is our
power. That is our glory. That is our mystery.*" [36]

At no other time during my slice of history was I
as aware of people's hunger for prayer than in the
60's.   And even though in that hunger many
became altogether dependent on artificially
induced states that ended in a kind of spiritual
obesity, nevertheless the hunger was there.   In
a single decade, people from every religious
scene and every facet of faith were able to pray
together and seriously look into each other's eyes

---

36   Catherine Doherty, *Soul of my Soul.* Madonna House Publications, Combermere ON, 2006, pgs. 27.

with some hope of unity and peace. It was a time of profound spiritual and emotional sincerity and a time of even more profound spiritual danger and peril.

Those of us who took the Christian tradition seriously eventually came back to a discipline of prayer which is rooted in the Judaeo-Christian scriptures and from which our own Catholic sacramental relationship with God flows. Firmly planted on that ground of Faith again we quite naturally found ourselves taking a new look at those old devotions that have flowered in our endearing Catholic garden of faith. Suddenly novenas and beads, vigil lights and statues and icons made all the sense in the world because now we could see it was about more than "little ole ladies" and private devotions. This childlike side of our Catholic tradition opens up a dimension of prayer that few of us remembered though it is at the very center of all Christian prayer, namely that " ... *prayer is born when the mystery of God and the mystery of man meet.*"[37]

Thus prayer is not only something we do or say, but it is something we eventually are meant to *become*! The "saying" and "doing" are like the stained glass windows in a marvelous cathedral which give a particular light to all the thoughts,

---

37   Catherine Doherty, Ibid.

words and deeds taking place within, the light of the Son of God Who is the prayer of the Father " ... *so that we might daily become more like Christ, so that we daily become the way to the Father ... so that we might ultimately say, 'It is no longer I who live, but Christ who lives in me'" (Gal 2: 20 RSV)*[38]

To see into this inner sanctum of our Catholic prayer tradition we must focus on the prayer of the Mother of Jesus. Her greatness, though it has many facets, is perhaps most astounding at that point of faith which we are all meant to enter eventually: when She *became* what she prayed! In all her life she prayed to never say No to God and so by the time She said to the angel of the Lord, *"let it be done to me,"*—*fiat* in latin—she became a prayer and was thus the first human being who could say, without reservation, " *I live now, not I, but Christ lives in me!"* (Gal 2: 20) But what does that mean for those of us who are not "virgin" as Mary was, who are not pure and undefiled spiritually or physically as She was?

Our union with Christ in prayer is not about virginity, or purity or being undefiled but it is about what happens when *"the mystery of God and the mystery of man meet."*[39] It is about the unfathomable mystery of the Son of God taking

---

38   Catherine Doherty, Ibid.
39   Catherine Doherty, Ibid.

on our flesh and then through that "flesh-ing" making us one with Himself and all humanity in the flesh so that we can become a prayer. Most of our praying, except for our liturgical or sacramental life, is the process of putting words on our heart's deepest longing, to be one with Christ. And that longing was born in us the day we were baptized. It has been put there by Christ Himself in Whom we were baptized. It is the longing He has to personally take into His own flesh, all our sorrows and tears, our joys and expectations, so that they become His and then His can become ours.

Praying is one of the ways we express that baptismal desire from our heart. And prayer is "answered" as we say our Yes to the mystery of the connection between Christ's humanity and our own, when we say Yes but cannot see, when we say Yes and do not understand, when we say Yes without any noticeable or magnificent change in our own life, when we say Yes because it was a Yes that made it possible for Him to take on our flesh and join us all to Him in the first place— the Yes of His Mother. That Yes to the mystery of Christ and us in the flesh, that Fiat, begins with prayer and ends with union.

> "The mystery of God becoming man and of man 'becoming God' meet in prayer: the prayer of the Son to the Father, and of man

to his Brother. By his Incarnation, the God-man was able to pray to the Father, and by our divinization in Christ, we are able to pray through Jesus Christ to God the Father. God and man are thus united in prayer, joined in the one prayer which is Jesus Christ. In him, man, too, become a prayer.

"Prayer is suffering. It is 'com-passion' (suffering with). Out of nowhere, the suffering of humanity will fill you and you are like one dead. You listen to the news, and you are the man who has been kidnapped by terrorists. You become the woman dying of cancer. The pain of the whole world is upon you. At this moment, you don't pray. You simply share the suffering. That is what it means to be a prayer.

"From another corner of the earth, you hear good news! You hear of a fiesta being celebrated, and you share the happiness. Suddenly you feel like dancing in the middle of the night. You feel that perhaps God is dancing with you.

"Sometimes you are empty. You look at yourself and say, 'What am I doing here?' You feel as if you are no good. Temptations assail you, and a thousand tongues of doubt lick you like flames. That is when you become a prayer for the doubtful.

"Sometimes you go into the depths of hell, a man-made hell, an atheistic hell where you can't move. You are the atheist. You identify with the atheists of the world. But you descend there of your own free will, out of love. Your identification is a prayer.

"A person who is a prayer is someone deeply in love with the Word, deeply in love with a Person. When you are in love with God, your head is plunged into your heart. It is the happiest time of your life. Of course, we use our minds as far as practical needs are concerned. The house gets cleaned. The duty of the moment is always there. Far from interfering with your life, being a prayer makes you very meticulous about doing little things well for the love of God. The detached, critical part of your brain that endlessly dissects and analyzes and rationalizes about matters of faith has gone into your heart. This is what it means to become a prayer.

"Prayer is being constantly in the presence of God ... Suddenly, you know he is always there ... As you pray about the living, the suffering, the doubting, and all these things,

God is there. Once he is there, all things are there, and you become a prayer."[40]

As we pray, gradually the foreignness of this union between us and Christ becomes familiar. Because we are holy? No! Because we are totally faithful now? No! Because our life has turned around completely? No! Why then? How?

It happens when we realize there is no other answer but that the *"chain of acts and events that runs from our first hour through our last ..., [that] what happens between birth and death is message, challenge, test, succor—all from his hands ..., [That] the God who made you, saved you, and will one day place you in his light, also directs your life ... "*[41]

It happens when we finally believe that " ... *you are one with Jesus ...All that is his is yours ... his breath in your breath, his heart in your heart, all the faculties of his soul in the faculties of your soul ... you have one breath with him, one soul, one life, one will, one mind, one heart ... He desires that whatever is in him may live and rule in you ... "*[42]

It happens when we begin to understand *"that in suffering there is concealed a particular power that draws a person interiorly close to Christ, a spe-*

40   Catherine Doherty, Ibid., pgs 24-26

41   Guardini, ob cit.

42   St. John Eudes, ob cit.

cial grace ... [a] profound conversion. A result of such a conversion is not only that the individual discovers the salvific meaning of suffering but above all that he becomes a completely new person. He discovers a new dimension, as it were, of his entire life and vocation ... Nevertheless, it often takes time, even a long time, for this ... to begin to be interiorly perceived. For Christ does not answer directly and he does not answer in the abstract this human questioning about the meaning of suffering. Man hears Christ's saving answer as he himself gradually becomes a sharer in the sufferings of Christ."[43]

It happens when we realize that when we were baptized we were given a "*personal, incommunicable vocation to reproduce in our own lives the life and sufferings and charity of Christ in a way unknown to anyone else who has ever lived under the sun. When I see my trials ... as the sacramental gift of Christ's love, given to me by God the Father along with my identity and my very name, then I can consecrate them and myself with them to God. For then I realize that my suffering is not my own. It is the Passion of Christ, stretching out its tendrils into my life ...* "[44] and this unimaginable union through our own everyday life, in the flesh, as we are right now, makes the "*soul dizzy with the wine of*

---

43 John Paul II, ob cit.
44 Merton, ob cit.

Christ's love and pour[s] that wine as strong as fire upon the whole world."[45]

It is the fire of the Resurrection! Our joy is complete!

---

45 Merton, ob cit.

Epilogue

Risen Lord Jesus, may we all come to know that from the moment of our Baptism the purpose and meaning of every event in our entire life is to be found in You and You alone, the Incarnate Son of God. May we all come to know that nothing will ever happen to us or ever has happened to us that does not somehow mysteriously join us both together "in the flesh" now in a personal union beyond all telling. May we come to know that whatever we endure, be it sorrow or joy, life or death, it only takes us deeper into Your Own Heart so that in, with and through You we too can enter into the suffering and joy of the whole world through our own, for we have become one with them in You!

*In humble thanksgiving for this baptismal gift, let us promise, with the help of Your grace, that from now until the end of our days, **we will seek from You and You alone, in Your life and Your life alone, the personal, moment-by-moment explanation and meaning of every event in our life, past, present and future, even our own sin and weakness.***

Let our prayer become that of Your Mother so that we too will know, in our very flesh, that I live now, not I, but You live in me.

Fiat.

Amen.

Other Madonna House Publications
by Catherine Doherty:

Poustinia: Encountering God in Silence, Solitude & Prayer

Sobornost: Experiencing Unity of Mind, Heart and Soul

Living the Gospel Without Compromise

Soul of My Soul: Coming to the Heart of Prayer

Dear Father: A Message of Love for Priests

Dear Seminarian: On Becoming a Shepherd of Souls

Available from **Madonna House Publications**
Toll free phone: 1-888-703-7110
Internet: **www.madonnahouse.org/publications**
2888 Dafoe Rd, RR 2, Combermere ON Canada K0J 1L0